The Foreplay Gourmet

VOLUME II

Over One Hundred
— *MORE* —
Outrageous Recipes
For Making Love

Other Books
Researched By
Chris Allen

1001 Sex Secrets Every Man Should Know

1001 Sex Secrets Every Woman Should Know

1001 Sex Secrets Everyone Should Know

*The Foreplay Gourmet: Over One Hundred
Outrageous Recipes For Making Love*

The Foreplay Gourmet

VOLUME II

Over One Hundred
— *MORE* —
Outrageous Recipes
For Making Love

Researched
by
Chris Allen

Published by
Creative Fire
Post Office Box 1089
Maggie Valley, North Carolina 28751-1089

ISBN: 0-9636454-4-7

Printed in the United States of America

Contents

	Preface	9
Appetizers For Him	Faux Pockets	13
	Nipple Stacks	14
	Irish Schwing	15
	High-Heeled Hello	16
	Der Flater-spouse	17
	Gingerotica	18
	Shavety First	19
	Drenched Desire	20
	Tattoosome	21
	Tonguing The Restless	22
Appetizers For Her	Grin-adine	25
	Forearm Foreplay	26
	Tongue and Groove	27
	Wick-edly Deceiving	28
	Airotica	29
	The Tempting Towel	30
	Licks & Lobes	31
	Eyebrows-al	32
	Meal of Fortune	33
	The Arctic Server	34
	The Love Glove	35
Appetizers For Both	Shadow Boinking	39
	Selfish Steam	40
	The Melting Bullseye	41
	T & T	42
	Ama-ready	43
Entrees For Him	Brew-topia	47
	The Cocoa Push-up	48
	Squeeze & Please	49
	The Frozen Jewels	50
	The Door-gasm	51
	Slumber-gasm	52
	The Windsor Boa	53
	Chin-tensity	54
	Rockerotica	55
	The Miner's Helmet	56
	Bazooka Blow	57
	Hollow Wood & Vine	58
	Nintend-o-gasm	59
	Magic Shellatio	60
	The Man-daid	61
	Fruit Left The Room	62
	Rising Sundae	63
	Fluff 'n Stuff	64
	Jell-atio	65
	Cheddar-gasm	66
	The Inverted Cane	67
	Fellatiogurt	68
	Palming The Gopher	69

	Carnal Apple	70
	AT&Tease	71
	Whopper-gasm	72
	The Tingling Typewriter	73
	B.J. Masterpiece	74
	Knee-ding The Cruller	75
	The Blueberry Swirl	76
	Extreme De Menthe	77
	Sweaterotica	78
	Aunt Good Time-a	79
Entrees For Her	Snow & Joe	83
	The Silk Worm	84
	Alpha-lingus	85
	Under-brush	86
	Seltzer-gasm	87
	Ohmygodimthumbing	88
	Chinese Field Goal	89
	"Safe" Sex	90
	Magic Shellingus	91
	A Thousand Paper Tongues	92
	Porn On The Swab	93
	The Pearl Escalator	94
	Rescuing The Captain	95
	The Electro-flex	96
	The Squeaky Eel	97
	Slits Melt Lick-her	98
	Pop Rotica	99
	Marshmallingus	100
	Tongue-kist	101
	The Minnesota Mindbender	102
	Mint Two-lip	103
	Polygraphoria	104
	The Crescent Flutter	105
	Eskimo-gasm	106
	Maraschino-gasm	107
	Philly-lingus	108
	Flower-gasm	109
	Popsiclingus	110
	Boxing The Compass	111
	Hitching To Milwaukee	112
	Strumming The Harp	113
	Pit-O-Honey	114
Entrees For Both	The Backyard Schwing	117
	Leonardo De Kinky	118
	Shirts & Skirts	119
	Ping Me A Love Pong	120
Desserts	The One-Eyed Ghost	123
	Tempera-chair Rising	124
	Laundromate	125
	The Satin Cylinder	126
	The Wheelbarrow	127
	Whambamthankyoumaamcorder	128

```
┌─────────────────────────────────┐
│                                 │
│     To Order Additional         │
│     Copies Of This Book         │
│     In The United States        │
│          Or Canada,             │
│        Call Toll-Free           │
│     1-800-444-PLAY              │
│                                 │
└─────────────────────────────────┘
```

Preface

If you don't have a sense of humor, GET ONE before you continue reading this book.

The sexual techniques described within are unusual, unique, some even downright bizarre. They were related to me over the past year by everyday people who, like most of us, are constantly looking for new ways to keep the variety and passion in their relationships.

Before you dive into "the good stuff," there are probably a few things we should get straight. First, more than any earth-shattering physical technique, the most important thing you can give your partner in the bedroom is respect. Nothing does more to create a sense of trust, security and, ultimately, an environment where they feel comfortable enough to try new things. If there's something in this book that you want to try, but your partner doesn't, respect their wishes and let it go. Guilt trips will get you nowhere. Also, when your partner feels they've been treated with respect, they're much more likely to honor your request sometime in the future. Be patient and everybody wins.

Second, these recipes are meant to serve as guides. Use your imagination and come up with your own variations. There is no "right" or "wrong" way to do anything when it comes to matters of personal preference.

Finally, always remember to show your partner you love them in ways outside of the bedroom. While sex is best with someone you love, it should never become the only expression of your love. Showing love for your partner in non-sexual ways takes a great deal of the pressure off your sexual encounters and allows you both to relax, let down your guard and have FUN.

Which is exactly what this book is all about!

Appetizers
For Him

Faux Pockets

1 man, clothed
1 woman, clothed
1 pair scissors
1 pair shorts with pockets, old

1. Prior to seeing man, cut pockets completely open.

2. Put on shorts, without panties.

3. When you and man are standing in a public place, such as a theater or restaurant, ask man to reach into your pocket for something (keys, change, etc.).

4. Note look on man's face as his hand makes a remarkable discovery.

5. When the two of you are seated side by side, encourage man to reach back into pocket and stimulate you with his fingers.

   Note: Most men will not need the additional encouragement referred to in step 5.

Nipple Stacks

1 man, clothing optional
1 woman, topless
2 dozen coffee straws

1. Sit in straight-backed chair.

2. Invite man to kiss, lick and gently suck on right nipple until it becomes erect.

3. Instruct man to balance a single coffee straw on nipple.

4. Man continues stacking straws, one on top of the other, until they eventually fall. Object of game is to see which nipple can hold the greatest number of straws.

5. Repeat steps 2 through 4 using left nipple.

Irish Schwing

1 man, naked
1 woman, naked
1 bar soap
1 piece yarn, 10 inches long
1 knife

1. Use knife to etch a circle around center of soap.

2. Tie one end of yarn around soap. Make sure yarn is set in circle and soap is held securely in place.

3. Invite man to take a shower with you.

4. Upon getting into shower, inform man that you prefer using "soap on a rope," and *he's* the rope.

5. Tie loose end of yarn around man's penis, where head meets shaft.

6. Take shower, lathering yourself and man quite frequently.

High-Heeled Hello

1 man, clothed
1 woman, naked
1 pair high heels

1. While man is out, strip completely naked and put on shoes.

2. Greet man at door.

3. Inform man you couldn't find an outfit to match these shoes, so you decided to wear nothing at all.

Der Flater-spouse

1 man, clothed
1 woman, clothed
1 beachball
1 pair scissors
1 bottle white glue

1. Make sure you're alone.

2. Locate air valve on beachball.

3. Using scissors, cut out air valve, leaving an inch of beachball material all the way around valve. Discard remaining portion of beachball.

4. Spread glue on underside of air valve and stick to your stomach, covering navel.

5. When glue is dry, put on shirt, hiding air valve.

6. Find man. Ask him if he has ever had sex with an inflatable women or blow-up doll,

7. When man says "no," lift up your shirt to reveal air valve.

Gingerotica

1 man, clothed
1 woman, clothed
1 gingerbread man
1 pretzel stick, small

1. Poke pretzel stick through gingerbread man where penis should be.

2. Tell man that gingerbread man represents him.

3. Slowly kiss, lick and simulate fellatio on gingerbread man.

Shavety First

1 man, clothing optional
1 woman, naked
1 can shaving cream
1 hand-held shaver, new

1. Remove shaver from package. Inside, there should be a "dummy blade," a plastic representation of a blade without an actual razor in it. Do not throw it away.

2. Attach real razor to shaver.

3. Draw bath, get in tub, apply cream and shave legs.

4. When done, replace real razor blade with "dummy" and reapply shaving cream.

5. Invite man into bathroom and ask him to shave your legs.

Note: This will significantly arouse man without the threat of any nicks, cuts or accidents.

Drenched Desire

1 man, clothing optional
1 woman, naked
1 nightgown, sheer

1. Take bath or shower.

2. When finished, do not dry yourself.

3. Put on nightgown.

4. Display "wet look" for man.

Tattoosome

1 man, naked
1 woman, clothing optional
1 temporary tattoo
1 washcloth, wet

1. Have man sit on edge of bed. Sit on floor in front of him.

2. Instruct man to pull skin of scrotum tight.

3. Wet tongue by holding washcloth over it and squeezing out water. Moisten scrotum with flat, open tongue.

4. Apply tattoo, holding in place for the required length of time as per package directions.

5. Once tattoo is in place, lovingly admire artwork.

Tonguing The Restless

1 man, clothing optional
1 woman, clothing optional

1. While kissing, pause and ask man to stick out his tongue as far as it will go. Tell him he cannot retract it until you say so.

2. Quickly flick the tip of your tongue along the length of man's tongue.

3. Form an "O" with your lips and move your mouth up and down on man's tongue, as if performing fellatio.

4. Suck man's tongue deeply into your mouth and gently bite down.

5. Repeat steps 2 through 4 until desired consistency of arousal.

Appetizers
For Her

Grin-adine

1 woman, naked
1 man, clothing optional
1 bottle grenadine
1 ice cube
1 drinking straw

1. Place bottle of grenadine in microwave and heat for approximately 30 seconds on full power. Make sure top is not on bottle, as these are usually made of metal.

2. Have woman lie on her stomach.

3. Sit beside woman and methodically rub and massage shoulders and back.

4. Dip straw into grenadine bottle and suck liquid up to top. Use tongue to block opening of straw, then quickly replace with finger. The straw should now be filled.

5. Withdraw straw from bottle and place on woman's back just above buttocks.

6. Glide straw up woman's back to neck, moving finger slightly off top of straw. Heated grenadine should flow over woman's spine.

7. Run ice cube down woman's spine. Using mouth and tongue, remove liquid from skin.

Forearm Foreplay

1 woman, clothing optional
1 man, clothing optional

1. Take woman's forearm in your hands.

2. Pretend this part of her body is her most sensitive erogenous zone.

3. Brush your lips over inside of woman's wrist.

4. Gently kiss woman's inner elbow.

5. Using fingers, delicately stroke skin running from woman's palm to inner elbow.

Tongue and Groove

1 **woman, naked**
1 **man, clothing optional**
1 **cup frozen yogurt, any flavor**
1 **tablespoon**

1. Have woman lie on her stomach.

2. Place one tablespoon of frozen yogurt on back of woman's right knee.

3. Using only your tongue, slowly guide frozen yogurt up woman's thigh and over right buttock to small of back. If yogurt slides off woman's body at any point, begin again from knee.

4. Upon reaching small of back, use mouth to remove yogurt.

5. Repeat steps 2 through 4 using back of left knee.

Wick-edly Deceiving

1 woman, clothed
1 man, clothed
2 dozen candles
1 flashlight

1. While woman is away, place candles strategically around the bedroom.

2. Light candles.

3. Turn off circuit breaker(s) so lights do not work throughout entire house.

4. When woman arrives, have flashlight in hand and tell her there's been a power outage.

5. Guide woman to the bedroom and let the soft candlelight work its magic.

Airotica

1 woman, naked
1 man, clothing optional
1 can compressed air, with straw nozzle

1. Have woman lie on her stomach.

2. Hold can over woman's feet. Straw should be approximately 2 inches away from toes.

3. Depress nozzle, sending bursts of air over woman's toes, arches and heels. Gradually move up to calves and thighs.

4. Glide can over buttocks, sending short bursts of air over woman's body.

5. Progress upward, paying special attention to spine and neck.

6. Have woman turn over on her back.

7. Begin again, starting with fingers and hands, working toward shoulders.

8. Position nozzle over nipples, stomach, legs and finally over feet again.

Note: Used for removing dust particles from computer equipment, cans of compressed air can be found at most office supply stores.

The Tempting Towel

1 woman, naked
1 man, clothed
1 bath towel

1. Wait until woman gets into shower.

2. Go into bathroom and quietly remove her towel from rack.

3. Place towel into dryer and turn on.

4. When woman finishes shower, turn off dryer and remove towel.

5. Greet woman in bathroom and wrap her in hot towel.

Licks & Lobes

1 woman, clothing optional
1 man, clothing optional
1 paintbrush, very small
1 shot peppermint schnapps

1. Have woman lie on her side, eyes closed.

2. Sit beside woman.

3. Dip paintbrush into schnapps and "paint" around the edge of woman's ear.

4. Reapply schnapps to brush and "paint" inside curve of woman's ear, finishing with lobe.

5. Set brush down and run tongue along "painted" area, pausing to apply gentle suction to edges and lobe. Continue until schnapps has been removed.

6. Repeat steps 3 through 5 on other ear.

Eyebrows-al

1 woman, clothed
1 man, clothed

1. Cover woman's face with delicate, gentle kisses.

2. Gently brush tip of tongue over woman's eyebrows. Begin from the center of forehead and work out toward temples. Remember: the less you touch her in this area, the more she will feel it.

3. Brush woman's eyelashes with tip of tongue. Do not touch eyelids.

4. Open lips slightly and place eyelashes between them. Slowly pull head back and let eyelashes slip through lips.

5. Repeat steps 2 through 4 until desired consistency of arousal.

Meal of Fortune

1 woman, clothed
1 man, clothed
1 Chinese meal, take out
1 fortune cookie
1 pair tweezers
1 pair scissors
1 piece paper, blank
1 pen

1. Pick up Chinese food for two. Get 3 or 4 fortune cookies. You only need one, but it's good to have extras in case they break.

2. Prior to arriving home, use tweezers to remove fortune from cookie.

3. Cut a slip of paper the same size and write your own personalized fortune. Some examples: "There is a relaxing back rub in your future," "Your future holds a tantalizing foot massage," "Prepare for a multi-orgasmic oral experience," etc.

4. Using tweezers, carefully insert personalized fortune into cookie.

5. Go home, enjoy meal, give woman the cookie and make fortune come true.

The Arctic Server

1 woman, naked
1 man, clothing optional
1 metal serving spoon, large

1. Place spoon in freezer for approximately 30 minutes.

2. Have woman lie on her stomach.

3. Using underside of chilled spoon, glide over woman's calves, thighs and buttocks.

4. Lay spoon at small of back.

5. Run spoon up spine and over neck, stopping at hairline.

6. Have woman turn over.

7. Glide spoon over sides of breasts, nipples, stomach, thighs and vagina.

Note: Do not apply spoon to any "wet" areas, as it could stick.

The Love Glove

1 woman, naked
1 man, clothing optional
1 oven mitt
1 bag cotton balls
1 bottle white glue

1. Open bag of cotton balls and glue them one by one on both sides of oven mitt. Wait at least 1 hour for glue to dry.

2. Have woman lie on her stomach.

3. Place "love glove" on your hand.

4. Sit beside woman. Slowly run glove up and down entire length of woman's body, barely letting cotton balls touch her. Pay special attention to neck, spine, buttocks, backs of knees and arches of feet.

5. Have woman turn over.

6. Again, run glove over entire length of woman's body, caressing face, neck, breasts, stomach, pubic area, thighs, ankles and feet.

   Note: Once used as "love glove," do not use oven mitt for cooking.

Appetizers
For Both

Shadow Boinking

1 man, naked
1 woman, naked
1 desk lamp

1. With man standing, position desk lamp approximately 4 feet behind him so his shadow is cast against wall.

2. Woman positions herself half-way between man and wall.

3. Without actually touching man, woman makes her shadow caress, stroke, kiss and lick man's shadow.

4. Switch positions. Repeat steps 1 through 3.

   Note: The closer you stand to lamp, the bigger your body parts appear on wall.

Selfish Steam

1 man, naked
1 woman, naked
2 towels, large
2 glasses wine

1. Plug bathtub drain.

2. Run cold water, covering bottom of tub.

3. Run very hot water through shower, filling bathroom with steam.

4. Wrap towels around your waists or sit on them.

5. Talk, enjoy wine and let steam revitalize you.

The Melting Bullseye

1 man, naked
1 woman, naked
1 candle, paraffin

1. Man lies face up on floor. Woman stands above him.

2. Woman lights candle.

3. Woman holds candle at least 3 feet above man's chest. She then lands at least 3 drops of melted wax on each of man's nipples.

4. Switch places. Repeat steps 1 through 3.

Note: Holding candle at least 3 feet above partner allows wax time to cool as it falls. Do not lower candle beyond this point.

T & T

1 man, clothed
1 woman, clothed
2 T-shirts, old
1 pair scissors

1. Using scissors, cut several small slits in both T-shirts.

2. Each of you puts on a T-shirt.

3. Taking turns, rip open any slitted section, passionately kissing and licking the newly exposed area.

Ama-ready

1 man, naked
1 woman, naked
1 bottle amaretto
1 shotglass

1. Man lies face down.

2. Woman pours amaretto into shotglass.

3. Woman dips finger into shotglass and traces a single letter on man's back.

4. Woman repeats step three until letters spell out message.

5. When man correctly identifies message, woman removes amaretto from man's skin using mouth and tongue.

6. Switch places. Repeat steps 1 through 5.

Entrees
For Him

Brew-topia

1 man, naked
1 woman, clothing optional
1 cup tea, hot

1. Have man lie on his back.

2. Kiss, lick and apply gentle suction to penis until erect.

3. Take full sip of hot tea. Do not swallow.

4. Press lips against head of penis.

5. Quickly take penis into mouth, being careful not to let tea spill out.

6. Keep head still for approximately 15 seconds, allowing man to fully experience heat sensation.

7. Perform fellatio, opening mouth slightly to let hot tea trickle down shaft of penis and over testicles. Repeat step 3 as necessary.

8. Continue until orgasm or desired consistency of arousal.

The Cocoa Push-up

1 man,
1 woman,
1 can chocolate syrup
1 plastic cup

1. Pour chocolate syrup into plastic cup.

2. Have man lie on floor, face up.

3. Kiss, lick and apply gentle suction to inner thighs and testicles until penis becomes erect.

4. Have man turn over and assume "push-up" position with arms extended. Make sure penis is at least five inches from floor.

5. Place plastic cup directly under penis.

6. Instruct man to do three push-ups, dipping penis into chocolate syrup.

7. Have man turn over on his back.

8. Perform fellatio.

9. Continue until orgasm or desired consistency of arousal.

> Note: Never allow man to dip penis into tin can or glass container; always use plastic cup.

Squeeze & Please

1 man, naked
1 woman, clothing optional
1 toothbrush
1 tube toothpaste

1. Have man lie on his back.

2. Liberally apply toothpaste to toothbrush.

3. Brush teeth for approximately one minute.

4. Do not rinse. Wipe excess foam from around mouth.

5. Take man's penis into mouth, allowing foam enough time to invigorate penis with cooling sensation.

6. Perform fellatio.

7. Continue until orgasm or desired consistency of arousal.

The Frozen Jewels

1 man, naked
1 woman, clothing optional
2 ice cubes

1. Have man lie on his back.

2. Using mouth and hands, stimulate penis.

3. Instruct man to tell you when he is about to reach orgasm.

4. When man is ready to climax, press ice cubes firmly against testicles.

The Door-gasm

1 man, clothed
1 woman, clothed
1 closet door
1 screwdriver, Phillips

1. Instruct man to remove doorknob and latch from closet door.

2. Have man get in closet.

3. Close door. Use foot to hold shut.

4. Instruct man to remove his pants and underwear.

5. Tell man to place penis through opening in door where knob used to be.

6. Using hands, gently stroke and massage penis until erect.

7. Kneel down, pressing knees against door to make sure it remains shut.

8. Alternate between fellatio and manual stimulation.

9. Continue until orgasm or desired consistency of arousal.

>   Note: Depending on height of doorknob, you may want to have something for man to stand on.

Slumber-gasm

1 man, naked and asleep
1 woman, clothing optional

1. While man is sleeping, gently roll him onto his back.

2. Get completely under the covers.

3. Take penis into mouth and preform fellatio.

4. When man awakens, instruct him not to move or look under covers. If he does, you will stop.

5. Continue until orgasm or desired consistency of arousal.

The Windsor Boa

1 man, naked
1 woman, clothing optional
1 silk necktie

1. Have man lie on his back.

2. Kiss, lick and apply gentle suction to thighs and testicles until penis becomes erect.

3. Wrap middle of necktie around base of penis--one revolution. Ends should be facing in opposite directions.

4. Pull both ends of necktie, tightening loop around penis. Have man tell you at what point this becomes uncomfortable.

5. Keeping both ends of necktie securely in your hands, perform fellatio.

6. When you sense man is about to have orgasm, stop oral stimulation and pull both ends of necktie. Loop will tighten, delaying orgasm.

7. Loosen necktie and resume fellatio.

8. Repeat steps 6 and 7 at least three times.

9. This time, when you sense man is about to have orgasm, do not tighten necktie. Allow man to have orgasm.

Chin-tensity

1   man, naked
1   woman, clothing optional
1   chin-up bar

1.   Have man stand and place both hands on chin-up bar.

2.   Kneel in front of man and perform fellatio.

3.   Instruct man to lift his legs and hang from chin-up bar when he is about to reach orgasm.

4.   When man's legs rise off ground, switch to manual stimulation.

5.   Instruct man to pull his chin up and over bar. Man should remain there for duration of orgasm.

Note: With all muscles in his body contracting, man's orgasm is significantly intensified.

Rockerotica

1 man, naked
1 woman, clothing optional
1 rocking chair

1. Have man sit in rocking chair, legs apart, heels resting on top of rockers.

2. Sit or kneel in front of chair.

3. Kiss, lick and apply gentle suction to thighs and penis until erect.

4. Using hands, grasp both ends of rocking chair arms.

5. Perform fellatio keeping head still, using hands to rock chair back and forth.

6. Continue until orgasm or desired consistency of arousal.

The Miner's Helmet

1 man, naked
1 woman, naked
1 keychain flashlight
1 piece tape, five inches long

1. With man standing, tape keychain flashlight to top of penis, as far back on shaft as possible.

2. Turn on flashlight.

3. Turn out all other lights.

4. Kneeling in front of man, kiss, lick and apply gentle suction to penis until erect. Light should illuminate your face.

5. Perform fellatio.

6. Continue until orgasm or desired consistency of arousal.

Bazooka Blow

1 man, naked
1 woman, clothing optional
1 piece bubble gum

1. Place bubble gum in your mouth and begin chewing.

2. Have man lie on his back.

3. Using tongue, push gum to back corner of mouth. Kiss, lick and apply gentle suction to thighs and penis until erect.

4. Bring bubble gum to front of mouth and place mouth approximately 3 inches over penis.

5. Blow bubble.

6. Do not seal off bubble. Instead, lower bubble onto head of penis and open mouth, thus inverting bubble and completely sheathing penis with gum.

7. Using forceful suction, lips and teeth, remove gum from penis.

8. Repeat steps 4 through 7.

9. Continue until orgasm or desired consistency of arousal.

Hollow Wood & Vine

1 man, naked
1 woman, clothing optional
1 tomato
1 knife

1. Have man lie on his back.

2. Kiss, lick and apply gentle suction to thighs and testicles until penis becomes erect.

3. Using knife, cut ends off tomato.

4. With palms flat, hold tomato between hands and place on head of penis.

5. Move hands back and forth, as if trying to start a campfire with sticks, while guiding tomato downward onto penis. Continue until tomato has cleared head of penis.

6. Grasping tomato firmly in one hand, move up and down shaft of penis.

7. Using mouth, stimulate penis head.

8. Continue until orgasm or desired consistency of arousal.

Nintend-o-gasm

1 man, clothed
1 woman, clothing optional
1 video game, with joystick

1. Inform man you have come up with a new way to play a video game.

2. Have man lie on floor, face up, feet towards television. Give him joystick controller.

3. Straddle or sit on man's chest, facing television. This should block his view.

4. Unzip man's pants, take out penis and use hands to stimulate until erect.

5. Tell man his penis will now be your joystick. Using the real joystick, man must imitate your moves while you play video game. Only when you score a certain number of points will you bring him to orgasm.

6. Start video game, pausing only to restimulate penis manually if erection begins to subside.

7. When desired number of points are scored, perform fellatio. If not, "game over."

Note: If video game requires a "fire" button, tickle scrotum to signal man.

Magic Shellatio

1 man, naked
1 woman, clothing optional
1 bottle "hard shell" ice cream topping
1 teaspoon butter or margarine
1 balloon, oblong

1. Fill balloon with water, tie stem and place in freezer for approximately 1 hour.

2. Remove balloon from freezer and rub with butter or margarine.

3. Holding balloon by stem, squeeze topping around sides of balloon. Continue until topping completely coats balloon.

4. Wait approximately 30 seconds, allowing topping to harden into a shell.

5. Rest balloon, stem end down, in sink. Using knife, puncture balloon and allow water to drain into sink. Peel balloon away from shell.

6. Have man lie on his back.

7. Place shell over penis and perform fellatio.

8. Continue until orgasm or desired consistency of arousal.

The Man-daid

1 man, naked
1 woman, clothing optional
1 adhesive-stripped bandage

1. Have man lie on his back, knees bent, legs slightly apart.

2. Apply bandage to scrotum. Each adhesive end should cover a testicle.

3. Kiss, lick and apply gentle suction to thighs and stomach until penis becomes erect.

4. Perform fellatio.

5. As man approaches orgasm, grasp middle of bandage firmly between forefinger and thumb.

6. When man reaches orgasm, immediately rip bandage from scrotum.

Fruit Left The Room

1 man, naked and in shower
1 woman, clothed

1. Wait for man to get in shower.

2. Hide all of man's underwear.

3. When man comes out of shower, pretend not to know what happened to underwear.

4. After man gets dressed, sans underwear, rub and fondle crotch several times throughout evening.

5. Unzip pants and use hand to stimulate penis.

6. Continue until orgasm or desired consistency of arousal.

Rising Sundae

1 man, naked
1 woman, clothing optional
1 can whipped cream
1 cherry

1. Have man lie on his back.

2. Kiss, lick and apply gentle suction to thighs, stomach and testicles until penis becomes erect.

3. Starting at base of penis, liberally apply whipped cream in straight line running up shaft to head.

4. Repeat step three until penis is covered to taste.

5. Place cherry on tip of penis.

6. Using mouth, remove cherry. Do not swallow.

7. With cherry in mouth, remove whipped cream from penis.

8. Continue until orgasm or desired consistency of arousal.

Fluff 'n Stuff

1 man, naked
1 woman, naked
1 jar marshmallow fluff

1. Lie face up on bed.

2. Liberally apply marshmallow fluff to breasts, concentrating on cleavage.

3. Have man straddle your waist and place penis between breasts.

4. Hold breasts together with hands, allowing only enough room for man's penis.

5. Have man move penis in and out of cleavage.

6. As man thrusts, lift head and try to remove marshmallow fluff from penis.

7. Apply additional fluff as needed.

8. Repeat steps 5 through 7 until orgasm or desired consistency of arousal.

Jell-atio

1 man, naked
1 woman, clothing optional
1 jello shooter, in paper cup
1 spoon

1. Have man lie on his back.

2. Kiss, lick and apply gentle suction to thighs, stomach and testicles until penis becomes erect.

3. Using spoon, cut circle in jello shooter approximately 1 inch in diameter and 1/2 inch deep. Remove with spoon and feed to man.

4. Turn jello shooter upside-down and place on head of penis.

5. Tear away paper cup. Be careful not to disturb shooter.

6. Lick around shaft of penis. Jello shooter should remain balanced on head.

7. Open wide and take entire shooter into mouth. Swallow gradually while performing fellatio.

8. Continue until orgasm or desired consistency of arousal.

Cheddar-gasm

1 man, naked
1 woman, clothing optional
1 can pasteurized process cheese spray

1. Have man lie on his back, knees bent, legs slightly apart.

2. Kiss, lick and apply gentle suction to thighs, stomach and testicles until penis becomes erect.

3. Spray a line of cheese along underside of penis, from base of shaft to head.

4. Turn your head sideways and delicately lick cheese from underside of penis.

5. Repeat steps 3 and 4.

6. Continue until orgasm or desired consistency of arousal.

The Inverted Cane

1 man, naked
1 woman, clothing optional
1 peppermint candy cane

1. Have man stand.

2. Kneeling, kiss, lick and apply gentle suction to penis until erect.

3. Moisten curved portion of candy cane with mouth and hook over penis.

4. Keeping penis inside hook, turn candy cane upside-down so it resembles a "J."

5. Grasp candy cane with thumb and forefinger where stem rises just above penis.

6. Move candy cane back and forth along shaft of penis, varying speed and intensity, while stimulating penis head with mouth.

7. Remoisten curved portion of candy cane and shaft of penis with mouth as needed.

8. Continue until orgasm or desired consistency of arousal.

Fellatiogurt

1 man, naked
1 woman, clothing optional
1 yogurt cone, any flavor

1. Have man stand, legs apart.

2. Touch top of yogurt cone to man's testicles and hold for approximately 10 seconds.

3. Using mouth and tongue, remove yogurt from testicles.

4. Kiss, lick and apply gentle suction to penis until erect.

5. Perform fellatio, pausing frequently to run yogurt up and down underside of penis.

6. Continue until orgasm or desired consistency of arousal.

Note: Use damp cloth to remove all yogurt residue before attempting intercourse.

Palming The Gopher

1 man, naked
1 woman, clothing optional
1 bottle baby oil

1. Have man lie on his back.

2. Stroke and caress thighs, testicles and penis until erect.

3. Place small amount of baby oil in palm.

4. Grasp shaft of penis with other hand.

5. Rub head of penis with oiled palm in clockwise, circular motion.

6. Reverse motion to counter-clockwise.

7. Repeat steps 5 and 6, reapplying oil as necessary.

8. Continue until orgasm or desired consistency of arousal.

Carnal Apple

1 man, naked
1 woman, clothing optional
1 caramel apple wrap

1. Have man lie on his back.

2. Kiss, lick and apply gentle suction to thighs, stomach and testicles until penis becomes erect.

3. Encircle penis with caramel apple wrap, pressing ends firmly together to secure.

4. Using teeth, perforate a circle in caramel apple wrap. Be careful not to bight down too hard.

5. Nibble away perforated caramel circle and perform fellatio on exposed area of penis.

6. Repeat steps 4 and 5 until orgasm or desired consistency of arousal.

AT&Tease

1 man, clothed, on telephone
1 woman, clothing optional
1 piece paper
1 pen

1. While man is seated and talking on telephone, write a note that says, "I'll only keep going as long as you keep talking."

2. Hand man note and unzip pants.

3. Take out penis and perform fellatio.

4. Continue until orgasm, desired consistency of arousal or man hangs up.

Whopper-gasm

1 man, naked
1 woman, clothing optional
1 malted milk ball

1. Have man lie on his back, knees bent, legs slightly apart.

2. Kiss, lick and apply gentle suction to thighs, testicles and penis until erect.

3. Place malted milk ball in mouth. Do not bite into it.

4. Take head of penis into mouth.

5. Using tongue, run malted milk ball around penis where head meets shaft, varying speed, direction and intensity.

6. Continue until orgasm or desired consistency of arousal.

The Tingling Typewriter

1 man, naked
1 woman, clothing optional

1. Have man lie on his back, legs stretched out.

2. Sit beside man.

3. Using fingertips, press head of penis against man's stomach.

4. Gently fondle testicles.

5. Starting at base of penis, flick tongue back and forth along underside of penis. Slowly move upward.

6. Upon reaching head of penis, run flattened tongue back down shaft in one, long stroke.

7. Repeat steps 5 and 6 until orgasm or desired consistency of arousal.

B.J. Masterpiece

1 man, naked
1 woman, clothing optional
1 bottle barbecue sauce
1 basting brush

1. Have man lie on his back.

2. Dip basting brush in barbecue sauce.

3. Brush sauce onto penis and testicles.

4. As penis becomes erect, brush sauce onto underside.

5. When genitals are sufficiently covered, use flat, open tongue to remove sauce from testicles.

6. Use mouth and tongue to remove sauce from penis.

7. Continue until orgasm or desired consistency of arousal.

Knee-ding The Cruller

1 man, naked
1 woman, legs bare
1 bottle hand lotion

1. Have man lie face up on floor.

2. Squeeze a small amount of lotion into palm.

3. Apply lotion to testicles and penis until erect.

4. Sit sideways next to man. Swing legs over man and place both feet on opposite side. Position backs of knees directly over penis.

5. Apply lotion to the inside portion of both calves, just under knee.

6. Extend legs, capturing penis between knees.

7. With both heels planted on floor, point right toe upwards. This will cause knee to bend.

8. Quickly alternate, pointing one toe out and the other up. Knees will move up and down, rubbing top of penis one way while simultaneously rubbing bottom the other.

9. Continue until orgasm or desired consistency of arousal.

The Blueberry Swirl

1 man, naked
1 woman, clothing optional
1 tablespoon blueberries, frozen

1. Have man lie on his back.

2. Kiss, lick and apply gentle suction to inner thighs, testicles and penis until erect.

3. Place frozen blueberries into mouth.

4. Perform fellatio. Using tongue, swirl blueberries around head of penis.

5. Continue until orgasm or desired consistency of arousal.

Extreme De Menthe

1 man, naked
1 woman, clothing optional
1 shotglass Creme De Menthe

1. Have man lie on his back.

2. Kiss, lick and apply gentle suction to thighs, testicles and penis until erect.

3. Take shot of Creme De Menthe and swirl around mouth.

4. Place mouth over penis and close. Using tongue, coat penis with Creme De Menthe.

5. Open mouth, still surrounding penis, and inhale deeply. Hold breath for 5 seconds, allowing man to experience cooling sensation. Exhale. Man will now feel warming sensation.

6. Perform fellatio, repeating steps 3 through 5 as necessary.

7. Continue until orgasm or desired consistency of arousal.

Sweaterotica

1 man, naked
1 woman, naked
1 Angora sweater, any color

1. Have man lie on his back.

2. Put on sweater.

3. Pull one sleeve of sweater down, covering hand.

4. Wrap sleeve-covered hand around penis and stimulate manually.

5. Continue until orgasm or desired consistency of arousal.

Aunt Good Time-a

1 man, naked
1 woman, clothing optional
1 bottle maple syrup

1. Have man lie on his back.

2. Warm maple syrup in microwave for approximately 30 seconds at full power.

3. Check syrup with finger, making sure it is not too hot.

4. Pour a thin stream of maple syrup onto penis, testicles and inner thighs.

5. Slowly lick syrup from inner thighs, then testicles.

6. Perform fellatio, using tongue to remove remainder of syrup from penis.

7. Continue until orgasm or desired consistency of arousal.

Entrees
For Her

Snow & Joe

1 **woman, naked**
1 **man, clothing optional**
1 **bowl ice, crushed**
1 **cup coffee, hot**

1. Have woman lie on her back, knees bent, legs apart.

2. Kiss, lick and apply gentle suction to inner thighs, bikini line and vagina.

3. Take full sip of hot coffee and keep in mouth approximately 15 seconds before swallowing.

4. Perform cunnilingus for 1 minute.

5. Place crushed ice in mouth for 10-15 seconds, making sure ice is in constant contact with tip of tongue.

6. Perform cunnilingus for 1 minute.

7. Repeat steps 3 through 6 until orgasm or desired consistency of arousal.

The Silk Worm

1 woman, naked
1 man, clothing optional
1 silk scarf, long
1 silk scarf, short

1. Using short silk scarf, blindfold woman. Have woman stand, legs slightly apart.

2. Stand at woman's side, facing her.

3. Place long silk scarf between woman's legs, holding one end behind her and the other in front.

4. Slide scarf back and forth along woman's calf, gradually moving up to thigh.

5. Raise scarf above woman's midsection. Continue sliding scarf back and forth, stimulating clitoris and vagina.

6. Have woman lie on her back.

7. Lay scarf over woman's vagina.

8. Using tongue and lips, stimulate clitoris and vagina through silk scarf.

9. Continue until orgasm or desired consistency of arousal.

Alpha-lingus

1 woman, naked
1 man, clothing optional

1. Have woman lie on her back, legs apart,

2. Kiss, lick and apply gentle suction to thighs, bikini line and vagina.

3. Trace circles around clitoris with tip of tongue.

4. Starting with the capital letter "A," use tongue to slowly lick the alphabet on and around clitoris.

5. Continue until orgasm or desired consistency of arousal.

Under-brush

1 woman, naked
1 man, clothing optional
1 pastry brush

1. Have woman lie on her back.

2. Make sure pastry brush bristles are clean and soft.

3. Gently run brush along inner thighs, bikini line and around perimeter of vagina.

4. Starting at bottom of vagina, glide brush along lips and over clitoris.

5. Repeat step 4 several times.

6. Duplicate the path of brush, this time using your tongue.

7. Lick and apply gentle suction to clitoris.

8. Alternate stroking vagina and clitoris with brush and tongue. Perform cunnilingus.

9. Continue until orgasm or desired consistency of arousal.

Seltzer-gasm

1 woman, naked
1 man, clothing optional
1 glass water
1 effervescent bicarbonate tablet

1. Have woman lie on her back, legs apart, knees slightly bent.

2. Break tablet into quarters.

3. Kiss, lick and apply gentle suction to inner thighs, clitoris and vagina.

4. Place the rounded edge of one quarter tablet between the top-most portion of vaginal lips. Only insert enough of the tablet to hold it in place.

5. Take small sip of water and hold in mouth.

6. Press your lips against the portion of vagina where tablet is located and let the water run out.

7. Perform cunnilingus, pausing frequently to repeat steps 5 and 6.

8. Continue until orgasm or desired consistency of arousal.

Note: Do not use tablets that contain aspirin or other medicines.

Ohmygodimthumbing

1 woman, naked
1 man, naked

1. Have woman lie on her stomach, legs slightly apart.

2. Insert right thumb into vagina.

3. Bend thumb rapidly. Repeat several times.

4. Clench remaining fingers of right hand into a tight fist.

5. Wrap four fingers of left hand around fist and gently insert left thumb into vagina, aligning it side-by-side with right thumb.

6. Alternate bending motion between both thumbs, varying speed and intensity based on woman's response.

7. Continue until orgasm or desired consistency of arousal.

Chinese Field Goal

1 woman, naked
1 man, clothing optional
1 pair chopsticks

1. Have woman lie on her back, legs apart, knees slightly bent.

2. Kiss, lick and apply gentle suction to inner thighs, bikini line, clitoris and vagina.

3. Roll pubic hair running along outside of left vaginal lip around one chopstick until taut.

4. Repeat step 3 with hair running along right vaginal lip.

5. Using chopsticks, gently pull lips apart and hold in place with one hand.

6. Using finger(s) of free hand, stimulate vagina. Use mouth and tongue to stimulate clitoris.

7. Continue until orgasm or desired consistency of arousal.

"Safe" Sex

1 woman, naked
1 man, clothing optional
1 slip paper
1 pen

1. Write three double-digit numbers on paper (for example, 56-43-65).

2. Inform woman you would like to engage in some "safe sex." Hand her the slip of paper, telling her that you think this is the combination to *her* safe.

3. Have woman lie on her back.

4. Moisten first two fingers of either hand with tongue and massage vagina. Inform woman you are now going to crack her safe.

5. Remoisten tip of first finger and trace circles clockwise around clitoris. Each rotation counts as "1" toward your combination.

6. After reaching the first number, reverse direction and count up to second number.

7. For third number, use your tongue.

8. Repeat steps 4 through 7 until orgasm or desired consistency of arousal.

Magic Shellingus

1 **woman, naked**
1 **man, clothing optional**
1 **bottle "hard shell" ice cream topping**
1 **teaspoon butter or margarine**
2 **balloons, round**
1 **knife**

1. Fill balloons with water, tie stem and place in freezer for approximately 1 hour.

2. Remove balloons from freezer and rub with butter or margarine.

3. Hold one balloon by stem and squeeze topping around balloon.

4. Continue application until topping has completely coated balloon.

5. Wait approximately 30 seconds, allowing topping to harden into a shell. Rest balloon, stem down, in sink. Using knife, puncture balloon and allow water to drain into sink. Peel balloon away from shell.

6. Repeat steps 3-5 with second balloon.

7. Have woman lie on her back and place both shells on breasts.

9. Lick edges of shells. Keeping melted topping on tongue, perform cunnilingus.

A Thousand Paper Tongues

1 woman, naked
1 man, clothing optional
1 telephone book
1 pillow

1. Have woman lie on her back.

2. Place pillow underneath buttocks, elevating vagina.

3. Instruct woman to close eyes and open legs wide.

4. Sit cross-legged between woman's legs and place telephone book in your lap.

5. Rotate telephone book so one corner is pointing directly at vagina, just above clitoris.

6. Using thumb, pull back bottom corner of telephone book. Moving thumb upward, allow pages to fall, fluttering against clitoris.

7. Repeat step 6 several times.

8. Continue until orgasm or desired consistency of arousal.

Porn On The Swab

1 **woman, naked**
1 **man, clothing optional**
2 **cotton swabs**
2 **rubber bands, small**
1 **pencil, unsharpened**
1 **bottle baby oil**

1. Lay cotton swabs across each other to form an "X" with about 1/4" between tips.

2. Wrap rubber band around center of "X."

3. Place pencil perpendicular between top of "X" and wrap rubber band around tips to hold pencil secure.

4. Dip two bottom tips in baby oil.

5. Have woman lie on her back, legs apart.

6. Place bottoms tips of "X" on both sides of clitoris.

7. Using one hand, form a tight circle around center of "X" just below pencil. Do this by curling first finger in, against base of thumb.

8. With free hand, rotate pencil clockwise. After 1 minute, reverse.

9. Continue until orgasm or desired consistency of arousal.

The Pearl Escalator

1 woman, naked
1 man, clothing optional
1 string of pearls

1. Have woman lie on her back, knees bent, legs slightly apart.

2. Sit between woman's legs.

3. With right hand, hold pearls parallel to vagina.

4. Lightly touch pearls to vagina. Using thumb, press pearls against vagina, just below clitoris. Thumb should be pointing at clitoris.

5. Using free hand, pull pearls upward, each bead stimulating clitoris.

6. Continue until orgasm or desired consistency of arousal.

Rescuing The Captain

1 woman, naked
1 man, clothing optional
1 wintergreen breath mint, with hole

1. Have woman lie on her back.

2. Kiss, lick and apply gentle suction to inner thighs, bikini line and abdomen.

3. Place mint in your mouth.

4. Kiss and lick vagina, giving mint time to partially dissolve.

5. Using finger, gently pull back hood, exposing clitoris.

6. Manipulate mint to tip of tongue.

7. Place mint on clitoris.

8. Gently suck on mint, drawing clitoris through hole.

9. Flick tongue back and forth over clitoris as lightly and rapidly as you can.

10. Draw mint back into mouth and repeat steps 5 through 9.

11. Continue until orgasm or desired consistency of arousal.

The Electro-flex

1 woman, naked
1 man, clothing optional
1 electric toothbrush

1. Have woman lie on her back, knees bent, legs slightly apart.

2. Kiss, lick and apply gentle suction to inner thighs, bikini line and vagina.

3. Moisten first two fingers with mouth and gently insert into vagina.

4. Flex fingers alternately while slowly rotating wrist.

5. Grasp electric toothbrush in free hand and turn on (always start at lowest speed setting).

6. Place smooth back of toothbrush against clitoris.

7. Continue until orgasm or desired consistency of arousal.

The Squeaky Eel

1 woman, naked
1 man, naked
1 bottle baby oil

1. Have woman lie on her back, legs apart.

2. Position yourself over woman in missionary-like fashion.

3. Do not attempt penetration. Instead, place penis on top of vagina, head pointing towards woman's navel.

4. Pour small amount of oil into palm of one hand.

5. Place palm flat on penis, pressing it firmly against vagina.

6. Thrust penis forward and back over clitoris. Repeat several times.

7. Continue until orgasm or desired consistency of arousal.

Slits Melt Lick-her

1 woman, naked
1 man, clothing optional
2 washcloths
1 bowl warm water
1 pair scissors

1. In middle of each washcloth, cut a 3" diagonal slit.

2. Place both washcloths in bowl of warm water.

3. Have woman lie on her back.

4. Ring out one washcloth and lay it over woman's pubic area. Slit should be directly above vagina.

5. Insert tongue into slit and perform cunnilingus.

6. As washcloth cools, repeat steps 4 and 5 using other washcloth.

7. Continue until orgasm or desired consistency of arousal.

Pop Rotica

1 woman, naked
1 man, clothing optional
1 bag "exploding" candy

1. Have woman lie on her back, knees bent, legs slightly apart.

2. Kiss, lick and apply gentle suction to inner thighs, bikini line, vagina and clitoris.

3. Open bag of "exploding" candy and sprinkle a generous amount on tip of tongue.

4. Press tongue against lips of vagina, moving upward to clitoris. Candy should "pop."

5. Perform cunnilingus, pausing to reapply "exploding" candy as needed.

6. Continue until orgasm or desired consistency of arousal.

Note: Some brands of "exploding" candy have tiny bits of chewing gum mixed in with them. Using this mixture will provide less-than-satisfactory results.

Marshmallingus

1 woman, naked
1 man, clothing optional
1 jar marshmallow fluff

1. Have woman lie on her back.

2. Liberally apply marshmallow fluff over woman's entire body, paying special attention to nipples, navel and bikini line.

3. Lick marshmallow fluff off woman's body. Deliberate flicks of the tongue are generally more stimulating than a flat-tongued motion. In some cases, you may alternate.

4. Leave marshmallow fluff on tongue. Perform cunnilingus.

5. Continue until orgasm or desired consistency of arousal.

Tongue-kist

1 woman, naked
1 man, clothing optional
1 orange, seedless

1. Peel orange and divide into sections.

2. Have woman lie on her back.

3. Hold one orange section approximately 3 inches above left breast. Squeeze juice onto nipple.

4. Using mouth and tongue, remove juice from breast.

5. Repeat steps 3 and 4 with right breast.

6. Squeeze juice from another section over stomach. Remove with mouth and tongue.

7. Repeat step 6 on thighs.

8. Gently wedge orange section between lips of vagina. Nibble away, gradually advancing to cunnilingus.

9. Continue until orgasm or desired consistency of arousal.

The Minnesota Mindbender

1 woman, naked
1 man, clothing optional

1. Have woman lie on her back, knees bent, legs slightly apart.

2. Kiss, lick and apply gentle suction to inner thighs, stomach, bikini line and vagina.

3. Sit beside woman, facing her. Your lips should run parallel to lips of vagina.

4. Have woman raise nearest leg over your shoulder.

5. With thumb of either hand, pull back hood, revealing clitoris.

6. Using tongue, moisten your lips.

7. Press your lips against both sides of clitoris.

8. Gently roll lips inward, covering your teeth, while raising head.

9. Repeat steps 7 and 8 several times, using tongue to remoisten lips as necessary.

10. Continue until orgasm or desired consistency of arousal.

Mint Two-lip

1 woman, naked
1 man, clothing optional
1 glass peppermint schnapps

1. Have woman lie on her back.

2. Pour small amount of peppermint schnapps into woman's navel.

3. Dip tongue in schnapps.

4. Using tongue, trace small circles around woman's right nipple.

5. Gently blow on right nipple, allowing woman to experience cooling sensation.

6. Repeat steps 3 through 5 with left nipple.

7. Again, dip tongue into schnapps.

8. Run tongue along both sides of vagina, then gently blow.

9. Repeat steps 7 and 8, this time using tongue on and around clitoris.

10. Perform cunnilingus, reapplying schnapps as necessary.

11. Continue until orgasm or desired consistency of arousal.

Polygraphoria

1 woman, naked
1 man, clothing optional
1 throw pillow, small

1. Have woman kneel, legs apart.

2. Lie on your back, behind woman, and position your head directly underneath vagina.

3. Place pillow under head.

4. Have woman lower herself until clitoris comes into contact with your pointed, outstretched tongue.

5. Instruct woman to ask you a "yes" or "no" question.

6. If answer is "yes," keep tongue still and nod head up and down. If "no," shake head side to side.

7. Continue nodding or shaking head until woman asks next question.

8. Continue until orgasm or desired consistency of arousal.

The Crescent Flutter

1 woman, naked
1 man, clothing optional

1. Have woman lie on her back, knees bent, legs slightly apart.

2. Place head between woman's legs.

3. Kiss, lick and apply gentle suction to inner thighs, stomach, bikini line and vagina.

4. Open mouth approximately 1/4 inch. Roll lips inward, covering teeth.

5. Press mouth against top of woman's vagina, clitoris between your lips.

6. Keeping lips curled inward, form a seal around area and apply gentle suction, drawing clitoris upward.

7. Dart tongue from side to side, barely touching clitoris.

8. Continue until orgasm or desired consistency of arousal.

Eskimo-gasm

1 woman, naked
1 man, clothing optional
1 Eskimo pie, on stick

1. Have woman lie on her back.

2. Unwrap Eskimo pie and glide over woman's outer thighs, stomach, breasts, nipples and inner thighs.

3. Bite tiny hole in chocolate covering at very top of Eskimo pie.

4. Turn Eskimo pie upside-down and hold approximately 4 inches above vagina.

5. As ice cream drips onto vagina, remove with tongue.

6. Lay Eskimo pie on woman just above clitoris and perform cunnilingus.

7. Continue until orgasm or desired consistency of arousal.

Maraschino-gasm

1 woman, naked
1 man, clothing optional
1 jar maraschino cherries, with stems

1. Have woman lie on her back.

2. Open jar. Use forefinger to hold lid off-center, creating a small opening that will only let cherry syrup out.

3. Pour small amount of cherry syrup over woman's breasts and stomach.

4. Using mouth and tongue, suck cherry syrup from woman's body.

5. Remove one cherry, stem intact, from jar.

6. Hold cherry between teeth and, bending over woman, glide cherry over vagina.

7. Using tongue, gently push cherry between lips of woman's vagina, being careful not to push it too deep.

8. Kiss, lick and apply gentle suction to clitoris.

9. Bite down on stem and remove cherry.

10. Repeat steps 6 through 9 until orgasm or desired consistency of arousal.

Philly-lingus

1 woman, naked
1 man, clothing optional
1 tub cream cheese, chilled

1. Have woman lie on her back.

2. Kiss, lick and apply gentle suction to inner thighs, stomach, bikini line and vagina.

3. Dip forefinger into cream cheese. Transfer from finger to tip of tongue.

4. Press tongue against clitoris. Remain still, allowing cold to stimulates clitoris.

5. Run tongue around clitoris, pausing to apply gentle suction. Reapply cream cheese as necessary.

6. Continue until orgasm or desired consistency of arousal.

Flower-gasm

1 woman, naked
1 man, clothing optional
1 rose, thornless

1. Have woman lie on her back.

2. Hold rose above woman's stomach. Glide rose over skin while simultaneously twirling back and forth between fingers.

3. Brush rose over breasts, cleavage, neck, face and arms.

4. Move down legs and twirl rose around woman's toes.

5. Stroke vagina with rose.

6. Pull one petal from rose and place on tip of your forefinger.

7. Gently press rose pedal against clitoris. Using finger, make "figure eights."

8. Keeping rose petal between finger and clitoris, vary speed, intensity and pattern based on woman's preference.

9. Continue until orgasm or desired consistency of arousal.

Popsiclingus

1 woman, naked
1 man, clothing optional
1 popsicle

1. Have woman lie on her back, knees bent, legs slightly apart.

2. Holding popsicle by stick, glide along breasts down to stomach.

3. Run popsicle down each leg.

4. Using tongue, remove melted popsicle from skin, starting at bottom of leg and working up to breasts.

5. Touch popsicle to vagina. Hold 5 seconds, then remove.

6. Use mouth and tongue to remove melted popsicle from vagina.

7. Repeat steps 5 and 6 until orgasm or desired consistency of arousal.

   Note: Never touch popsicle to partner's skin immediately after it has come out of freezer. Always wait at least 3 minutes, giving popsicle surface time to warm up.

Boxing The Compass

1 woman, naked
1 man, clothing optional

1. Have woman lie on her back, knees bent, legs slightly apart.

2. Kiss, lick and apply gentle suction to inner thighs, bikini line and vagina.

3. Position tongue on top of clitoris.

4. Swing tongue downward and left in half-circle, stopping at bottom of clitoris. Motion should resemble an open parenthesis.

5. Retrace movement from bottom to top.

6. Repeat steps 4 and 5. Tongue should move quickly from top to bottom and back up.

7. Position tongue at top of clitoris and move downward and right, stopping at bottom of clitoris. Motion should resemble a closed parenthesis. Repeat steps 5 and 6.

8. Continue, switching sides, until orgasm or desired consistency of arousal.

> Note: Most women are more sensitive on one side of their clitoris. This technique will help you determine which side.

Hitching To Milwaukee

1 woman, naked
1 man, clothing optional
1 bottle baby oil

1. Have woman lie on her back, knees bent, legs slightly apart.

2. Kiss, lick and apply gentle suction to inner thighs, stomach, bikini line and vagina.

3. Make a fist. Stick thumb out as if hitchhiking.

4. Apply a tiny amount of baby oil to the middle knuckles of all four fingers (the same knuckles you would use to knock on a door).

5. Line up knuckles parallel with vagina.

6. Gently touch clitoris with knuckle of forefinger,

7. Move wrist upward so all four knuckles brush clitoris. Reverse motion so knuckles brush clitoris again on downstroke. Repeat rapidly.

8. Continue until orgasm or desired consistency of arousal.

Strumming The Harp

1 woman, naked
1 man, clothing optional

1. Have woman lie on her back.

2. Sit beside woman, facing her.

3. Lift woman's nearest leg and rest it on your shoulder.

4. Line up fingers of one hand so tips run parallel to vagina. Forefinger should be over clitoris.

5. Gently tap fingers (as if impatient) against vagina.

6. Moisten tip of forefinger with mouth and trace circular patterns around clitoris.

7. Repeat steps 5 and 6 until orgasm or desired consistency of arousal.

Pit-O-Honey

1 woman, naked
1 man, clothing optional
1 peach, large
1 knife

1. Using knife, core peach. Cut top and bottom portion of peach away from pit.

2. Place pit in mouth and suck for approximately 1 minute. This both smooths and warms pit.

3. Have woman lie on her back, knees bent, legs apart.

4. Remove pit from mouth and hold between thumb and forefinger. Dull, rounded end of pit should *always* be facing out.

5. Glide pit along vaginal lips.

6. Using short strokes, gently rub pit against one side of clitoris, then the other.

7. Repeat steps 5 and 6 until orgasm or desired consistency of arousal.

Entrees
For Both

The Backyard Schwing

1 man, naked
1 woman, naked
1 tree, large
1 motorcycle tire
1 coil of rope, 50 feet long

1. Cut rope into three 10-foot lengths.

2. Throw remaining 20-foot length of rope over sturdy branch of tree and tie *securely*.

3. Lay tire on ground directly under rope.

4. Loop a 10-foot strand through tire and rope hanging from tree so one end of tire is 12-15 inches above ground.

5. Repeat step 4 with two remaining 10-foot strands. Position rope into a triangle, suspending tire evenly above ground.

6. Woman sits in middle of tire.

7. Man lies on ground, penis under vagina.

8. Upon penetration, man rotates tire. Rope tension should lift woman above penis. Upon release, tire spins back in opposite direction. Woman should be lowered onto penis, then lifted again.

9. Continue until orgasm or desired consistency of arousal.

Leonardo De Kinky

1 man, naked
1 woman, naked
1 jar fudge topping

1. Woman lies on her back and pours fudge topping into navel.

2. She then asks man to "paint" a picture on her stomach using penis as brush.

3. Man dips head of penis into fudge and proceeds to paint picture, reapplying fudge as necessary.

4. Woman cleans "brush" with her mouth. Man cleans "canvas" with his.

5. Man kneels above woman's head and positions penis over her mouth.

6. Woman performs fellatio.

7. Man leans over and, using tongue, licks fudge topping off woman's stomach. Man performs cunnilingus.

8. Continue until orgasm(s) or desired consistency of arousal.

Shirts & Skirts

1 man, clothed
1 woman, clothed

1. Set one rule: both of you can do whatever you desire, but you *cannot* remove clothing.

2. For the man: zipper can be unzipped, but penis cannot be taken out.

3. For the woman: panties may be pulled to one side, but must remain around waist. Dress may be unzipped in back, but arms must remain in sleeves.

4. For both: only the top 3 buttons of a shirt or blouse may be unbuttoned.

5. No cheating. Be creative. Continue until orgasm(s) or desired consistency of arousal.

Ping Me A Love Pong

1 man, naked
1 woman, naked
1 ping pong ball

1. Woman lies on her back.

2. Man rests ping pong ball in woman's navel.

3. While woman tries to remain still, man performs whatever techniques he thinks will cause her to writhe or squirm with pleasure.

4. Man continues until ping pong ball rolls out of navel.

5. Switch places and repeat from step 1.

    Note: If ping pong ball rolls out of navel, then back in, you must continue.

Desserts

The One-Eyed Ghost

1 man, naked
1 woman, naked
1 sheet, old
1 pair scissors

1. Cut hole in center of sheet, approximately 3" in diameter.

2. Man lies on his back. Woman completely covers him with sheet.

3. Woman places hole over penis.

4. With penis now being the only part of the man that is visible, woman mounts man and inserts penis into vagina.

5. After 3 minutes of intercourse, woman grasps one side of sheet and man to rolls over on top of her.

6. Man makes sure woman is completely covered with sheet. Vagina should be the only visible part of woman.

7. Resume intercourse for another 3 minutes.

8. Repeat steps 4 through 6 until orgasms.

Tempera-chair Rising

1 man, naked
1 woman, naked
1 chair, straight-backed
1 bath towel

1. Fold towel into quarters and place on seat of chair.

2. Woman faces back of chair and kneels on towel, legs slightly apart.

3. Standing behind woman, man inserts penis into vagina.

4. During intercourse, man massages woman's thighs, buttocks and breasts.

5. Continue until orgasm(s) or desired consistency of arousal.

Laundromate

1 man, naked
1 woman, naked
1 washing machine

1. Set washing machine to "rinse and spin" cycle.

2. Woman sits on top of washer, facing front, legs apart.

3. Man penetrates woman, starts machine and commences intercourse.

4. Continue until orgasm(s) or desired consistency of arousal.

The Satin Cylinder

1 man, naked
1 woman, naked
1 satin nightshirt
5 bath towels
2 shoelaces

1. Lay one towel on floor and roll it length-wise.

2. Roll another towel around the first.

3. Continue until all five towels are rolled into one.

4. Place bundle into satin nightshirt.

5. Tie shoelaces tightly around bundle at both ends.

6. Woman kneels down on all fours and straddles bundle.

7. Man enters woman from behind.

8. Woman spreads knees outward. Clitoris should rub against bundle as man thrusts forward.

9. After woman reaches orgasm, adjust position so man's testicles brush bundle when thrusting resumes.

10. Continue until orgasm.

The Wheelbarrow

1 man, naked
1 woman, naked

1. Woman kneels on floor and leans forward, resting on forearms.

2. Man kneels behind woman and inserts penis into vagina.

3. Man wraps forearms around woman's thighs and slowly stands up. Penis should remain in vagina.

4. Woman straightens legs, places palms on floor and extends arms, pushing herself up.

5. Resume intercourse.

6. Continue until orgasm or desired consistency of arousal.

Whambamthankyoumaamcorder

1 man, naked
1 woman, naked
1 video camera

1. Make love in a variety of positions for 2 minutes at a time. Man holds camera for first minute, woman for second.

2. After both of you have reached orgasm, hook camera up to television and see what making love looks like from your partner's point of view.

3. Go at it again.